Have you ever stood outside at night and looked up at the sky? Watching the night sky is a lot like going on a treasure hunt in the dark. The longer you look, the more things you can find!

The moon is the easiest treasure to spot. It's usually the biggest and brightest light in the night sky. From night to night, the moon seems to change shape. Sometimes it's huge and round. Other times it's a tiny sliver.

The moon's different shapes are called **phases**. What phase of the moon do you see on page 2?

(You can't see it!)

new moon

crescent moon

quarter moon

gibbous moon

full moon

What if you could fly to the moon?
You would see that it's covered with
giant craters and valleys. From Earth,
these craters and valleys look like dark
and light spots.

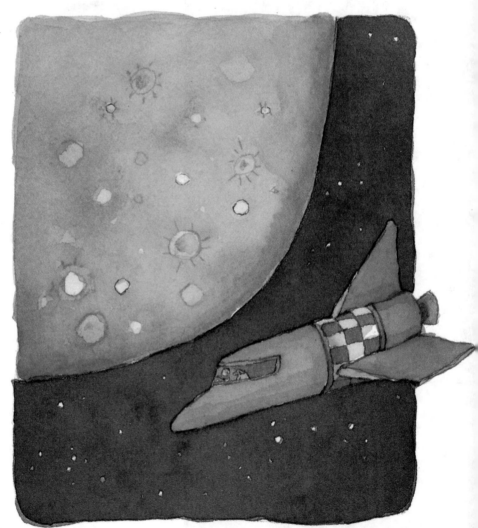

Some people look at these dark and light spots and see a person's face. Other people see an animal when they look at the moon. What do you see?

Around the moon are millions and millions of stars. Long ago, people saw that the stars made shapes in the sky. They imagined they saw pictures in these shapes.

They saw dragons and snakes, hunters and heroes. These star pictures are called constellations. What pictures do you see in this sky?

Different constellations appear in the sky at different times of the year. But you can almost always find the Big Dipper. It looks like a giant ice cream scoop. Nearby is the Little Dipper.

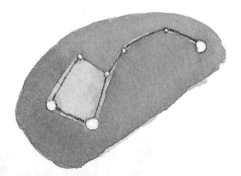

This is what the Little Dipper looks like. Can you find the stars that make its shape on the next page?

Orion, the Hunter, comes out in the dark winter sky. Three bright stars make Orion's Belt. Close by is Taurus, a bull that Orion is chasing.

This is what Taurus looks like. Can you find the stars that make its shape on the next page? (Hint: Look for the cluster of seven stars on Taurus's back.)

The moon and stars aren't the only treasures in the night sky. Sometimes you can see a planet. Venus is the easiest to find. It's often the first bright speck of light to appear in the evening.

Watch closely and you might see bright lights streaking through the sky. We call these "shooting stars," but they aren't stars at all. They're meteors. Meteors are bits of burning dust or rock. How many meteors do you see here?

If you're lucky, one night you may spot a comet. Comets are huge chunks of dust and ice that appear in the sky. They look like they have long tails.

On the darkest nights, the sky twinkles and sparks with billions and billions of lights. So step outside on the next clear night, and look up! What treasures can you find?